Simple Rules for Money

ALSO BY JAMES A. HARNISH

Strength for the Broken Places

You Only Have to Die:
Leading Your Congregation to New Life

Journey to the Center of the Faith:
An Explorer's Guide to Christian Living

Passion, Power, & Praise:
A Model for Men's Spirituality from the Life of David

Simple Rules for Money

John Wesley on Earning, Saving, & Giving

James A. Harnish

Abingdon Press
Nashville

SIMPLE RULES FOR MONEY
JOHN WESLEY ON EARNING, SAVING, AND GIVING

Copyright © 2009 by Abingdon Press

This book is printed on acid-free, elemental chlorine-free paper.

CIP data has been applied for.

Scripture quotations in this publication, unless otherwise indicated, are from the New Revised Standard Version of the Bible, copyright © 1989, Division of Christian Education of the National Council of the Churches of Christ in the United States of America. All rights reserved.

Scripture marked *The Message* are from *THE MESSAGE.* Copyright © Eugene H. Peterson, 1993, 1994, 1995, 1996, 2000, 2001, 2002. Used by permission of NavPress Publishing Group.

Scripture marked (NIV) are taken from the Holy Bible, NEW INTERNATIONAL VERSION®. Copyright © 1973, 1978, 1984 by International Bible Society. All rights reserved throughout the world. Used by permission of International Bible Society.

Those marked KJV are from the King James or Authorized Version of the Bible.

ISBN: 978-0-687-46616-0

09 10 11 12 13 14 15 16 17 18—10 9 8 7 6 5 4 3 2 1
MANUFACTURED IN THE UNITED STATES OF AMERICA.

Contents

1. When Crisis Forces Change

An excellent branch of Christian wisdom is... namely, the right use of money—a subject largely spoken of by men of the world; but not sufficiently considered by those whom God hath chosen out of the world.... Neither do they understand how to employ it to the greatest advantage.

JOHN WESLEY, "THE USE OF MONEY"

Read: Luke 16:1-18.

WHAT DOES IT TAKE for you to make a radical change in the way you earn, save, and spend your money?

There are times when I can identify with the man who came home from work one day to discover a small magnetic sign on the front of the refrigerator that said *Prayer changes things.* Immediately he took it down. His wife, offended by what appeared to be the man's lack of faith, asked, "What's wrong with you? Don't you like prayer?" He shot back, "Sure, I like prayer. I just don't like change."

If we are ruthlessly honest, most of us don't like change, particularly when it comes to our finances. We crave economic stability and financial security. We measure success by the size of our bank account and the profitability of long-term investments. We save for a secure retirement and are frightened when signs of political insecurity send the stock market into a tailspin. We don't like change, particularly when it comes as a result of forces over which we have little or no control.

When British Prime Minister Gordon Brown said that "sometimes it's a crisis that forces change," he pointed to an underlying reality that faces us every time we are forced to make difficult decisions about money.[1]

- A spouse is fired, retires, or dies.
- A child is born or goes to college.
- A plant shuts down, and a position is eliminated or a salary reduced.
- An investment turns out to be an unanticipated windfall or a dismal failure.
- The global economy shifts downward in a major recession.

How do we deal with a financial crisis that calls for fundamental change in the way we earn, invest, and spend our money? On a deeper level, what would be required for us to experience a fundamental shift in the relationship between our faith and our finances? We like prayer; we just don't like change. What difference does our relationship with Christ make in the way we use our money?

> There's something here also for seasoned men and
> women,
> still a thing or two for the experienced to
> learn—
> Fresh wisdom to probe and penetrate,
> the rhymes and reasons of wise men and
> women.
> PROVERBS 1:5-6, THE MESSAGE

Wisdom from Wesley

The eighteenth century was a time of major economic and social change in England. The gap between the comfortable, affluent aristocracy and the beleaguered, poverty-stricken working class was growing larger and more tenuous. One historian described the era as having a "taut, neurotic quality—the fantastic gambling and drinking, the riots, brutality and violence, and everywhere and always a constant sense of death."[2] John Wesley confronted the crisis of his time with a word of hope for transformation in every area of human experience. The personal and spiritual discipline that he practiced and taught resulted in people becoming more responsible, better educated, and more prosperous. Soon Wesley faced the unexpected predicament of Methodist people accumulating wealth, wearing fine clothing, and building more attractive preaching-houses.

In response, Wesley called for a fundamental change in the relationship between faithful Christian people and their money, when he wrote his classic sermon "The Use of Money." The result was useful not only in his own time but also through the present day, providing a corrective balance to the two extremes that sometimes seem to be the only alternatives for Christian people.

At one extreme are the "prosperity gospel" preachers who tell us that God wants everyone to be rich. They promise that faithfulness to the gospel will result in financial success. They use the Bible as a "get rich quick" scheme that generally results in the preachers getting rich, whether or not any of their followers do. The size of their congregations, the ratings of their television programs, and the place their books hold on the best-seller lists confirm that there is always a market for their dubious theology.

At the opposite extreme are the preachers who approach the subject of money as if they were afraid of being infected with a fatal disease. Reacting against the abuses of the "prosperity" preachers and in response to people who (sometimes for good reason) complain that all the church wants is their money, they act as if the gospel has nothing to say on the subject, in spite of the fact that Jesus talked more about money and possessions than any other subject except the Kingdom of God.

In an attempt to convey a spirit of pious poverty, some preachers approach the subject of money apologetically as if they are embarrassed that it even needs to be mentioned while people in their congregations wrestle with these matters day in and day out. The result is often that Christian people live with a total disconnect between the faith they celebrate in worship on Sunday morning and the financial decisions they make every day of the week.

I recently preached on John Wesley's sermon, which includes Wesley's instruction to "gain all you can." When I met with a small group of businesspeople the following Monday, they said it was the first time they had heard anything like it. Their experience had been that the church looked down on any desire to gain wealth and that the only word the gospel had for rich people was that there was more chance of a camel getting through the eye of a needle than there was for them to get into heaven. As a result, these businesspeople lived for years with inner tension between their faith in Christ and their desire to prosper in their work. Wesley's words created the opportunity for them to discover a new connection between their finances and their faith.

After nearly four decades of pastoral ministry, my conviction is that that while most people are wary of "prosperity gospel" preachers who promise that God will make them rich, and while many people are weary of preachers who use biblical texts only as a fund-raising tool for their ministries and programs, most faithful people are ready to receive a biblical word that will guide them toward a healthy connection between their finances and their faith. Particularly in times of economic crisis and change, they are searching for that gift of God that the writer of Proverbs summed up in a single word: *wisdom.*

Exceptional Wisdom for Unexceptional People

Old Testament scholar Ellen Davis identifies Proverbs as "a book for unexceptional people trying to live wisely and faithfully in the generally undramatic circumstances of daily life."[3] Biblical wisdom is more than the accumulation of knowledge or information; it is a gift of the Spirit of God that enables us to know what to do with the knowledge we accumulate in order to live well in our relationships with God and one another.

Eugene Peterson captured the spirit of biblical wisdom in his paraphrase of the opening verses of the Proverbs:

> These are the wise sayings of Solomon,
>   David's son, Israel's king—
> Written down so we'll know how to live well and right,
>   to understand what life means and where it's going;
> A manual for living,
>   for learning what's right and just and fair;
> To teach the inexperienced the ropes
>   and give our young people a grasp on reality.
>   PROVERBS 1:1-4, *THE MESSAGE*

Biblical wisdom on the relationship between faith and finances goes beyond fund-raising for the church, although Paul unashamedly sets the biblical model for that task in his letters to the Christians in Corinth. Based on Paul's example, no preacher needs to be cautious or embarrassed about challenging Christian disciples to give to the work of God's Kingdom!

But at its core, biblical wisdom on the use of money is centered on helping faithful people order their financial lives around their faith in God so that they can live well in every area of their lives. The writer of Proverbs promises that when we honor God with whatever we own and give God our first and best, our "barns will be filled with plenty, and (our) vats will be bursting with wine" (Proverbs 3:5-10).

Jesus may have been drawing on the wisdom of Proverbs when he spoke about money and possessions. He assured his followers that when we order our lives around the reign and rule of God, then "these things will be given to you as well" (Luke 12:31).

Money, the Excellent Gift

When John Wesley wrote his sermon "The Use of Money," he picked up the word *wisdom* from Proverbs when he identified "the right use of money" as "an excellent branch of Christian wisdom." He went on to acknowledge that the wise use of money is "widely discussed among people in the world" but that it is "not sufficiently considered by those whom God hath chosen out of the world." He recognized the need for faithful people to give more attention to "the use of this excellent talent" and "how to employ it to the greatest advantage."

Wesley chose as his text Jesus' strange command to "make to yourselves friends of the mammon of unrighteousness" (Luke 16:9 KJV). It's an odd enough text, taken from an even more peculiar parable. Jesus shocked his disciples—and he shocks us!—with the story of a crooked manager who, when confronted with a financial crisis, was smart enough to look out for his own welfare (Luke 16:1-9). Here's the way Eugene Peterson paraphrased the punch line of the parable.

> Now here's a surprise: The master praised the crooked manager! And why? Because he knew how to look after himself. Streetwise people are smarter in this regard than law-abiding citizens. They are on constant alert, looking for angles, surviving by their wits. I want you to be smart in the same way—but for what is right—using every adversity to stimulate you to creative survival, to concentrate your attention on the bare essentials, so you'll live, really live, and not complacently just get by on good behavior.
>
> LUKE 16:8-9, THE MESSAGE

The parable is followed by Jesus' stern application of the story to the relationship between our faith and our finances.

> If you're honest in small things,
>   you'll be honest in big things;
> If you're a crook in small things,
>   you'll be a crook in big things.
> If you're not honest in small jobs,
>   who will put you in charge of the store?
> No worker can serve two bosses:

He'll either hate the first and love the second
Or adore the first and despise the second.
You can't serve both God and the Bank.
LUKE 16:10-13, THE MESSAGE

It's a parable with a twist; a story that turns our expectations inside out. The crook becomes the hero because of the way he managed his money. And that's precisely the kind of twist that Wesley built into his sermon.

In contrast to the preachers who railed against money as "the grand corrupter of the world, the bane of true virtue, the pest of human society," Wesley reminded his followers that "the *love* of money," not money itself, is "the root of all evil" (1 Timothy 6:10). "The fault," he said, "does not lie in the money, but in them that use it." He declared that when used in ways that are consistent with biblical wisdom, money is "an excellent gift of God, answering the noblest ends." He called money "a most compendious instrument of transacting all manner of business, and (if we use it according to Christian wisdom) of doing all manner of good."

While some pretentiously pious people think of money as "filthy lucre," it would be difficult to find a nobler vision for money than the one John Wesley gives:

> In the hands of his children, it is food for the hungry, drink for the thirsty, raiment for the naked.... By it we may supply the place of an husband to the widow, and of a father to the father-less; we maybe a defence for the oppressed, a means of health to the sick, of ease to them that are in pain. It may be as eyes to the blind, as feet to the lame; yea, a lifter up from the gates of death![4]

Three Plain Rules

Wesley laid out what he called "three plain rules" for the wise use of money: Gain all you can. Save all you can. Give all you can.

The first two of those rules led to improved productivity among the Methodist people, resulting in increased income. As they grew more prosperous and began to rise out of the lower economic classes, Wesley became concerned that their success might separate them from the people they were called to serve. That concern led him to a more aggressive emphasis on the third rule, "Give all you can." We can almost hear the urgency in his voice when Wesley declared, "Let not any man imagine that he has done anything, barely by going thus far, by 'gaining and saving all he can,' if he were to stop here. All this is nothing, if a man go not forward, if he does not point all this at the farther end."

Two-and-a-half centuries later, Wesley's rules on the use of money continue to provide practical and positive wisdom for discovering a faithful, biblical, and hopeful approach to our financial lives. The rules are time-tested, experience-proven disciplines that if practiced over time can lead to a healthy relationship between our faith and our finances. They provide the framework for a radical change in the way we earn, invest, and use our money.

> Happy are those who find
>   wisdom,
>   and those who get
>   understanding.
> PROVERBS 3:13

To set the stage for our exploration of Wesley's rules, let's look at the process by which faithful people confront a crisis that causes change.

C. Douglas Lewis, the retired president of Wesley Theological Seminary, was writing for leaders in theological education when he affirmed that "a crisis can become a gift" by serving as a "wake-up call" for us to examine how we function.[5] To help us look at the process by which we can confront economic change, I've borrowed the "crucial elements" that Lewis described in his article and am presenting them here as issues for all of us to consider: clarity of mission, persistent core values, and a commitment to excellence.

Clarity of Mission

Who am I? Why am I here? What are the most important commitments and priorities in my life? How do my financial decisions grow out of my identity as a follower of Jesus Christ? Clarity of mission defines who we are.

In his sermon "The Use of Money" and his companion sermon "The Danger of Riches," Wesley began with the assumption that Christians would be different from the people around them because their financial decisions would be a direct result of their identity as disciples of Jesus Christ. For Christian disciples, the first question is not *How much do I have?* but rather *Who am I?*

Jesus wrestled with these questions of identity and mission during the forty days he spent in the wilderness at the beginning of his ministry (Luke 4:1-13). Satan tempted him, beginning each time with the words "If you are the Son of God...." The temptations dealt with very practical issues of power, prestige, and purpose in Jesus' life, questions that had to be settled before Jesus could set out to fulfill his mission in the world. These are still the fundamental questions that define who we are and why we are here.

When plenty of money is available, it's easy for any of us to start believing that we can do anything and have everything we want. We are tempted to assume that our identity is defined by the size of our house, the make of our car, the label on our clothing, and the balance in our checkbook. But when money is tight, when finances are precarious, when we cannot have everything we want, then we are forced to face deeper questions with ruthless honesty. The crisis becomes an opportunity to take a serious inventory of the things that are most important in our lives.

Like Jesus wrestling with Satan in the wilderness, we feel pain when forced to confront the deepest questions of our identify and personal mission. But as Jesus discovered, there is no escape if we intend to be faithful to God's claim on our lives. This is the non-negotiable starting point for dealing with fundamental change.

> God is solid backing to a well-lived life,
> But he calls into question a shabby performance.
>
> PROVERBS 10:29, *THE MESSAGE*

Persistent Core Values

If our mission defines *who* we are, our values define *what* we will or will not do in a particular situation. Wesley placed specific boundaries around his directive to "gain all you can." Those boundaries are defined by the core values by which he believed the followers of Christ should live.

Paul defined the core values of the Christian life when he challenged the Christians in Ephesus to "lead a life worthy of the calling to which you have been called" (Ephesians 4:1). He affirmed the positive side of that challenge by reminding them of "the hope of their calling." Then he offered this warning:

> You must no longer live as the Gentiles live, in the futility of their minds. They are darkened in their understanding, alienated from the life of God because of their ignorance and hardness of heart. They have lost all sensitivity and have abandoned themselves to licentiousness, greedy to practice every kind of impurity. That is not the way you learned Christ! For surely you have heard about him and were taught in him, as truth is in Jesus. You were taught to put away your former way of life, your old self, corrupt and deluded by its lusts, and to be renewed in the spirit of your minds, and to clothe yourselves with the new self, created according to the likeness of God in true righteousness and holiness. (Ephesians 4:17-24)

Paul applied the values of their new life in Christ to their economic decisions when he wrote: "Thieves must give up stealing;

rather let them labor and work honestly with their own hands, so as to have something to share with the needy" (Ephesians 4:28).

Here's an extreme contemporary example that would be consistent with the examples in Wesley's sermons. There is a lot of money to be gained by stealing, but doing so would contradict the core values of personal morality by which a Christian person is called to live. Unfortunately, the challenges we face are generally not that clearly defined. The values by which we live must be worked out in complex and often subtle choices we make each day. But consistent commitment to Christ-defined values frames the boundaries within which we decide what we can and cannot do.

A Commitment to Excellence

If mission defines *who* we are, and values define *what* we do, then a commitment to excellence defines *how* we will use the gifts, talents, and opportunities we have been given.

> The lazy do not roast their game, but the diligent obtain precious wealth.
>
> PROVERBS 12:27

In his sermon "The More Excellent Way," John Wesley described the way Christians, "after using some prayer," should "apply themselves to the business of their calling." His sermon could be an eighteenth-century version of Tom Peters's business best seller *In Search of Excellence*.

Wesley declared that "it is impossible that an idle man can be a good man—sloth being inconsistent with religion." The result was that the early Methodists become known for the diligence and quality of their work. Then he asked the deeper question, "For what end do you undertake and follow your worldly business?"

He acknowledged that providing for a person's basic needs and the needs of the family is "a good answer as far as it goes; but it does not go far enough.... A Christian may go abundantly farther." He said that the end or goal of labor "is to please God... to do the will of God on earth as angels do in heaven.... Is not this 'a more excellent way'?"[6] He went on to challenge his followers to combine their work and their piety.

> In what *manner* do you transact your worldly business? I trust, with diligence, whatever your hand findeth to do, doing it with all our might; in justice, rendering to all their due, in every circumstance of life; yea, and in mercy, doing unto every man what you would he should do unto you. This is well: But a Christian is called to go still farther—to add piety to justice; to intermix prayer, especially the prayer of the heart, with all the labour of his hands. Without this all his diligence and justice only show him to be an honest Heathen.[7]

Finally, Wesley called his followers to do their work in the spirit of Christ. "If you act in the Spirit of Christ you carry the end you at first proposed through all your work from first to last... continually aiming, not at ease, pleasure, or riches... but merely at the glory of God. Now can anyone deny that this is the most excellent way of pursuing worldly business?"[8]

> A slack hand causes poverty,
> but the hand of the diligent
> makes rich.
>
> PROVERBS 10:4

John Wesley's brother Charles expressed the commitment to excellence in the form of a hymn.

> Forth in thy name, O Lord, I go,
> my daily labor to pursue;
> thee, only thee, resolved to know
> in all I think or speak or do.

The task thy wisdom hath assigned,
O let me cheerfully fulfill;
in all my works thy presence find,
and prove thy good and perfect will.

For thee delightfully employ
what e'er thy bounteous grace hath given;
and run my course with even joy,
and closely walk with thee to heaven.[9]

George Eliot, the nineteenth-century British novelist who used a male pen name to make sure that her writing would be taken seriously, wrote a poem about the world-renowned violin maker Antonio Stradivari. In the poem, a young, undisciplined painter named Naldo mocks Antonio's hard work, telling him that he could have wealth and fame with a lot less labor. Antonio defends his work as being to the glory of God, saying that generations to come will use Stradivarius violins and be grateful. Antonio tells Naldo, "Not God Himself can make man's best / Without best men to help Him."[10]

It's possible that the work ethic of the Methodist home in which Eliot was raised had some influence in her description of Stradivari's sense that his work was to the glory of God. In any case, the Wesleyan emphasis on excellence continues to be an important element in the process by which we face the inevitable crisis that results in change.

Journalist Nancy Gibbs sounded a little like a preacher when she wrote, "Sometimes we change because we want to: lose weight, go vegan, find God, get sober. But sometimes we change because we have no choice.... It may take a while before we notice that those are often the changes we need to make most."[11]

Wesley's words on money provide the practical framework for changes that some of us most need to make.

2. Gain All You Can: A New Opportunity

We ought to gain all we can gain, without buying gold too dear, without paying more for it than it is worth.

JOHN WESLEY, "THE USE OF MONEY"

Read: Luke 12:13-34

GRADUATION SPEECHES by politicians and movie stars make their annual appearance in the news with the same regularity as spring flowers breaking through the soil, but high school valedictorians don't generally make headlines. Jem Lugo's speech, however, became the stuff of online news reports and Internet bloggers when it was rejected by the principal at Springstead High School in Spring Hill, Florida.

Jem, with a 3.98 grade average and a confirmed place in the freshman class at Harvard University, decided to skip all the polite graduation platitudes that "gush about these lofty, inspirational concepts that are supposed to make you feel all warm and gooey inside." Instead, Jem determined that she would shoot straight with her fellow seniors and remind them of "some basic concepts you can actually apply to your life."

Unfortunately, her first draft was a little more down-to-earth and irreverent than the principal could handle. The principal made Jem rewrite her speech. Having read both speeches, I can assure you that the speech that got rejected was more interesting (and a lot more fun!) than the one she delivered.

Here's the first piece of advice Jem gave to her fellow grads in the rejected speech. "First off," she said, "get money. You can't do anything without money. Do something with your life where you're able to have a steady, reliable source of income. Gamers, I'm sorry, but farming for gold in World of Warcraft [a video game] is not considered a reliable or socially acceptable source of income."[1]

My guess is that Jem had no idea she was channeling the voice of the eighteenth-century leader of Methodism. But when John Wesley laid out what he called "three plain rules" for the use of money, the first rule was "Gain all you can." The Jem Lugo version is "Get money!"

Get Money

Wesley identified "Gain all you can" as "the first and great rule of Christian wisdom with respect to money." Just as Jem Lugo told her classmates to do something with their lives that would provide a steady, reliable income, Wesley expected his followers to get to work and make a living. In no uncertain terms, he told them how to do it.

> Gain all you can by honest industry. Use all possible diligence in your calling. Lose no time. If you understand yourself and your relation to God and man, you know you have none to spare. If you understand your particular calling as you ought, you will have no time that hangs upon your hands. Every business will afford some employment sufficient for every day and every hour. That wherein you are placed, if you follow it in earnest, will leave you no leisure for silly, unprofitable diversions. You have always something better to do, something that will profit you, more or less. And "whatsoever thy hand findeth to do, do it with thy might." Do it *as soon* as possible: No delay! No putting off from day to day, or from hour to hour. Never leave anything till tomorrow, which you can do today. And do it *as well* as possible. Do not sleep or yawn over it: Put your whole strength to the work. Spare no pains. Let nothing be done by halves, or in a slight and careless manner. Let nothing in your business be left undone if it can be done by labour or patience.[2]

Whew! That kind of work ethic could wear out even a recovering workaholic like me! It's no wonder that the early Methodists became productive and prosperous. But if Jem Lugo was channeling Wesley, it's possible that Wesley was channeling the writer of Proverbs.

> Go to the ant, you lazybones;
>   consider its ways, and be wise.
> Without having any chief
>   or officer or ruler,
> it prepares its food in summer,
>   and gathers its sustenance in
>   harvest.
> How long will you lie there,
>   O lazybones?
> When will you rise from your
>   sleep?
> A little sleep, a little slumber,
>   a little folding of the hands to
>   rest,
> and poverty will come upon you
>   like a robber,
>   and want, like an armed
>   warrior.
>   PROVERBS 6:6-11

Wesley's instruction to "gain all you can" might seem obvious to those of us who have been conditioned by the mind-set of an upwardly mobile, high-achieving, success-driven, consumer-oriented culture. It's at the heart of what is often called the "Protestant work ethic" and is good advice for anyone interested in career advancement.

But when we slow down long enough to think about it, we know that in our high-stress, high-anxiety, high-cost culture, gaining all you can becomes a very complicated deal. There is both a good side and a shadow side to this principle. We saw evidence of the dark side in the crash of the global economy early in the twenty-first century.

A Look on the Dark Side

Everyone agrees with the diagnosis. The infection that landed the United States economy in the intensive care unit in the fall of 2008 and spread like a virus to the rest of the world was virulent greed. From top to bottom, as long as everyone was making money on sometimes questionable economic assumptions, some of the brightest and best people in the country kept drinking from the same contaminated well, ignoring every warning of an infection that would finally bring the patient, desperate for a cure, to collapse. Even then, the financial physicians couldn't agree on the proper treatment but finally began prescribing large doses of "bail out" money in the hope that the treatment would not be worse than the disease.

> The greedy person stirs up strife,
>   but whoever trusts in the LORD
>   will be enriched.
>
> PROVERBS 28:25

Novelist and PBS radio host Kurt Andersen wrote of the crisis, "Don't pretend we didn't see this coming." He pointed to the ways we started "living large literally as well as figuratively." He compared American consumers to Las Vegas gambling addicts who were on a winning streak that we thought would go on forever. Andersen said, "We knew, in our heart of hearts, that something had to give [but]... no one wanted to be a buzz kill." Then the crash came. Andersen compared the United States economy to the *Road Runner* cartoon character Wile E. Coyote, racing across the desert at max speed until he found himself suspended in mid-air off the edge of the cliff: "Economic gravity reasserted itself, and we plummeted."[3]

In telling his followers to "gain all you can," John Wesley acknowledged that he was speaking "like the children of the world." He said, "We meet them on their own ground." Lifted out of context, Wesley's words sound like an eighteenth-century version of Gordon Gekko's declaration "Greed is good!" in the 1987 movie classic *Wall Street*. In fact, "gain all you can" was the economic mantra of the American consumer culture for at least two decades. As long as everyone was making money, the disease continued to spread, but the symptoms of the infection were easy to see.

Phil Roughton is a pastor and longtime friend who leads a congregation on the upscale side of Fort Lauderdale, Florida. He was heading out the door of his favorite Starbucks when he nearly collided with a very attractive young woman coming in. He couldn't miss the fact that she had stepped out of an expensive convertible and looked as if she had just finished a photo shoot for a glossy fashion magazine. She was wearing a brilliant red, designer-labeled T-shirt with small, tasteful white letters that read *I want everything*.

Phil said that most of us, though we might hesitate to wear that T-shirt, "may have substituted greed for moral restraint.... When that happens, some end up with far more than they need to live—and the resulting 'What do you get for the person who has everything' dilemma, unique to our culture—while others don't have near enough."

Wesley knew the gravitational reality we work so hard to ignore. He knew that a lust for everything without boundaries or limitations is like Wile E. Coyote running toward the cliff.

> A thick bankroll is no help when life falls apart,
> But a principled life can stand up to the worst.
> PROVERBS 11:4 *THE MESSAGE*

Wise Warnings

While meeting the world on its own terms, Wesley spent most of his sermon "The Use of Money" putting up warning signs along the highway toward economic prosperity. His central theme can be captured in one sentence: "It is our bounden duty to do this: We ought to gain all we can gain, without buying gold too dear, without paying more for it than it is worth." Jesus gave the same warning when he said, "Take care! Be on your guard against all kinds of greed; for one's life does not consist in the abundance of possessions." Eugene Peterson paraphrased that verse to say, "Protect yourself against the least little bit of greed. Life is not defined by what you have, even when you have a lot" (Luke 12:15 *The Message*).

To make his point, Jesus told the story of a rich farmer whose land began to produce a bumper crop. Don't miss the fact that the farmer was already prosperous. He started out with more than he needed and ended up with more than his barns could contain. Even in difficult economic times, that could be an accurate personification of the United States economy in comparison to the rest of the world. What would the already-prosperous farmer do with his new-found prosperity?

In telling us what the farmer decided, Jesus said the farmer "thought to himself." In other words, the entire conversation took place inside the farmer's head. In narcissistic overconfidence, the farmer debated his situation without regard to anyone else, much less to God. He didn't consult a family member, business consultant, tax attorney, or investment advisor.

The farmer asked himself, "What should I do, for I have no place to store my crops?" He answered himself by deciding to pull down his barns and build bigger ones where he could store all his goods. You could say that Jesus' story was a biblical version of the recent boom in the personal storage business or of the fact that the average size of an American home has become larger while the average family has become smaller. Like the farmer, we need more and more space to store more and more stuff. In the story, the farmer told his soul, "Soul, you have ample goods laid up for many years; relax, eat, drink, be merry."

The Foolish Farmer

Gordon Gekko would have called the farmer a success. The farmer might have made it to the cover of *Fortune* magazine and become a cable news network personality. Many people would say that he had achieved "the American dream." He had it all! But God gave a different verdict. God said, "You fool! This very night your life is being demanded of you. And the things you have prepared, whose will they be?"

Parenthetically, "Whose will these things be?" is a very good question. It is, in fact, a question we need to answer. I am constantly amazed at the huge percentage of faithful, church-going people who do not have a will or estate plan. By default, they are giving the government the authority to answer that question for them. It's not foolish to save for the future and to prepare a will. Far from being foolish, preparing for the end of life is a critically important part of faithful Christian stewardship. But that's not the point of this parable.

The point of this parable is that it's foolish to live as if we are defined by how much we own.

It's foolish to assume that the point of earning money is to accumulate more money.

It's foolish to think only of ourselves and not to consider the impact our financial decisions have on others.

It's foolish to try to manage our money with no reference to God.

It's foolish to think that we can satisfy our soul with material possessions.

It's foolish to be so consumed by things that are temporary that we miss out on things that are eternal.

It's foolish to gain all we can at too high a price.

> The lips of the righteous feed many,
> but fools die for lack of sense.
> PROVERBS 10:21

The Danger of Riches

Jesus said the farmer was foolish. The farmer also was sick. He was infected with a terminal illness called "greed" or "covetousness." That's the biblical diagnosis of a person who has everything he or she needs—and then some—but continues to be driven by an insatiable desire for more.

In his sermon "The Danger of Riches," John Wesley described people infected by the disease of greed as those who "desire to be rich, to have more than *food* and *coverings*; they that seriously and deliberately desire more than food to eat, and raiment to put on, and a place where to lay their head, more than the plain necessaries and conveniences of life." By Wesley's definition, the disease could infect almost anyone who reads this book!

A preacher friend in California told me he had observed two strains of the disease of covetousness. Type A is an overwhelming desire to possess things that belong to other people at all costs. My friend observed that it generally infects underprivileged people who see what someone else has—or what marketing firms convince them they need to have—and are willing to do anything, including stealing, to get it.

Type B is more insidious and even more dangerous because it's so easy to miss. That's because the symptoms generally mask themselves as success. Type B covetousness is the uncontrollable desire to accumulate wealth even when you already have more than you need. People infected with it no longer control their possessions; their possessions control them.

I've found at least two mutations of the ailment. One is *affluenza*, defined as the constant and insatiable desire to accumulate more and more stuff. Affluenza has also been called the "sudden-wealth syndrome." If we tell the truth, it may be the disease most of us would love to have. But it is a dysfunctional or unhealthy relationship with wealth and the pursuit of it. When one person said that the only cure for affluenza is turning away from self, it sounded like something Jesus would have said.

Adam Hamilton diagnosed another mutation of the sickness of greed as *credititis*—the "buy-now-pay-later" addiction to an unhealthy use of credit cards. Credititis has spread like an epidemic through our culture.[4] The symptoms are staggering:

- 78 percent of American households (84 percent of the student population) have credit cards.
- At the end of 2008, the average outstanding credit card debt for households that have a credit card was $10,679.
- The average credit-card-indebted young adult household spends 24 percent of its income on debt payments.[5]

> Such is the end of all who are
>   greedy for gain;
>   it takes away the life of its
>   possessors.
> PROVERBS 1:19

In the sixteenth century, Martin Luther gave a slightly different diagnosis of the rich farmer's ailment. He used a Latin phrase borrowed from St. Augustine, *homo incurvatus in se*. The literal translation is "man curved in on himself." Luther wrote: "Our nature...is so deeply curved in on itself that it not only bends the best gifts of God towards itself...but it also fails to realize that it so wickedly, curvedly, and viciously seeks all things, even God, for its own sake."[6] The Greek philosophers portrayed the effects of *homo incurvatus in se* in the myth of Narcissus. He was so good-looking that the god Nemesis cursed him to fall in love with his reflection. The more Narcissus looked at himself, the smaller he became until there was nothing left but a little white flower. Eugene Peterson wrote, "He had starved to death on a diet of self."[7]

Like every mutation of the disease of greed, *homo incurvatus in se* is deadly. Life turned in on itself gets smaller and smaller until there is nothing left that can be called life. And Jesus said,

"So it is with those who store up treasures for themselves but are not rich toward God."

Life Is More

The parable of the foolish farmer created the setting for some of Jesus' most memorable teaching. He said that "life is more than food, and the body more than clothing." In contrast to the farmer who built bigger barns, Jesus spoke about the birds that have neither barns nor rented storage units, but are fed by God. He pointed to the lilies of the field, which neither toil nor spin, but are better dressed than a king. He reminded us that we are more valuable to God than birds or lilies. He challenged us to seek first the Kingdom—the reign and rule of God in human experience—in the confidence that if we get our lives in line with God's priorities, we will have everything else we need.

These teachings of Jesus constitute some of the most familiar passages in Scripture. Lifted out of context, I've seen them on everything from embroidered pillowcases to needlepoint wall hangings. But in their biblical setting, they serve as Jesus' antidote for the disease of greed. They are Jesus' alternative to the approach taken by the rich farmer. They are Jesus' warning to folks who think their lives are defined by their possessions. They are Jesus' cure for *homo incurvatus in se.*

Jesus' call to seek first the Kingdom of God is rooted in the wisdom of the Proverbs.

> Trust in the LORD with all your
> heart,
>   and do not rely on your own
>   insight.
> In all your ways acknowledge
> him,
>   and he will make straight your
>   paths.

Honor the Lord with your
substance
and with the first fruits of all
your produce;
then your barns will be filled
with plenty,
and your vats will be bursting
with wine.

PROVERBS 3:5-6, 9-10

The parable of the foolish farmer and the wisdom of Proverbs provide the biblical basis for John Wesley's rules on how to "gain all we can without paying too great a price for it."

Wesley calls us to gain all we can, but not at the expense of our health. He warns us not to "begin or continue in any business which necessarily deprives us of proper seasons for food and sleep."

That's a disturbing word for addicted workaholics like the author of this book! But it is a warning many need to hear. While some of us face the challenge of the high cost of living, others are paying too high a price for the cost of high living. Too many of us are allowing our drive to "gain all we can" to destroy our physical health. Far too many of us are working ourselves to death for the sake of money.

Wesley challenges us to gain all we can without damaging our souls. He puts a boundary around anything that would damage our spiritual and mental health. "We must preserve, at all events, the spirit of a healthful mind," Wesley says, by not participating in any "sinful trade." Wesley's list of "sinful trades" is specific to his time, but the issue he raises continues to mutate in every generation.

A salesman I know was making a lot of money in the telecommunications business. Then a corporate merger resulted in his company becoming the primary provider of pornographic movies for hotel room televisions. The conflict between his work and his Christian values created an ethical and economic crisis in his life. After intensive soul-searching and prayers, he determined that he could not live with his soul and keep on doing that job. He left a very lucrative position to take a job that did not pay nearly as well. While John Wesley never could have imagined the technology, he clearly understood the inner conflict my friend faced and would have supported the decision he made.

Wesley instructs us to gain all we can without hurting our neighbor. At the center of both the gospel and Wesley's theology is the "great commandment" to love God and to love our neighbor. Wesley said that obedience to the second commandment prevents us from doing injury to our neighbor in "substance" (anything that unfairly impacts another's economic stability), "body" (anything that injures the neighbor's health), or "soul" (anything that contributes to another person's sin).

The wisdom of Proverbs warns the reader about evil people who entice us to "waylay some harmless soul" in order to "get all sorts of valuable things and fill our houses with plunder" at another person's expense (Proverbs 1:10-16 NIV). Paul wrestled with a similar issue in his letter to Corinth when he wrote, "When you thus sin against members of your family, and wound their conscience when it is weak, you sin against Christ" (1 Corinthians 8:12).

As John Donne expressed in poetry, we are not islands to ourselves. We are part of one another. The way we earn our money has a direct impact on the lives of others. We cannot be faithful followers of Jesus Christ if we earn all we can by doing harm to our neighbors.

This piece of wisdom becomes even more complex in a global economy when we realize that it applies not only to the neighbor next door, but also to our neighbors around the world. We've seen the disturbing statistics that measure the contrast between American greed and the world's need.

- 20 percent of the world's people account for 86 percent of total private consumption.

- Americans constitute 5 percent of the world's population but consume 24 percent of the world's energy.
- We eat 815 billion calories of food each day, roughly 200 billion more than needed—enough to feed 80 million people.
- We throw away 200,000 tons of edible food daily.
- Our average individual daily consumption of water is 159 gallons, while more than half the world's population lives on 25 gallons.[8]

Friends in ministry in South Africa are quick to remind me that when the United States economy gets a cold, the South African economy comes down with pneumonia. It's a fact of life and death that overconsumption by the richest people in the world is stealing resources from the poorest.

And then there are the hauntingly prophetic words of President Dwight D. Eisenhower, warning us about the impact of our unrestrained military spending.

> Every gun that is made, every warship launched, every rocket fired signifies, in the final sense, a theft from those who hunger and are not fed, those who are cold and not clothed. This world in arms is not spending money alone. It is spending the sweat of its laborers, the genius of its scientists, the hopes of its children. This is not a way of life at all in any true sense. Under the cloud of threatening war, it is humanity hanging from a cross of iron.[9]

We are intricately bound together in this global economy and cannot be faithful to Christ if we gain all we can by doing damage to our neighbors, wherever they are.

John Wesley acknowledged the complexity in these issues. The choices are not easy. He said we should be "continually learning, from the experience of others, or from your own experience, reading, and reflection, to do everything you have to do better to-day than you did yesterday. And see that you practise whatever you learn, that you may make the best of all that is in your hands."

But amid the complexity of our times, my sense is that the greatest temptation among overachieving, ambitious, upwardly mobile folks is to ignore the price we are paying for our wealth until we are confronted with a physical, emotional, or spiritual crisis. Perhaps the new thing God wants to do in us is to help us rethink our personal and economic priorities rather than wait for crisis to force change.

A corporate executive was forced, like so many other professionals, to take an "unpaid furlough" from his office to help balance the company books. He told me that the crisis in his career caused him to rethink his overcommitment to work. He decided to find a better balance between his hours at the office and his hours with his children. He joined a men's Bible study group. The crisis in his work created the opportunity to find a healthier balance in his life.

So, what might Wesley's word be for us today?

Gain all you can by working at it. Do your best with every opportunity you are given. Use the talents, opportunities, and resources you have to their greatest and most productive effect. Biblical wisdom consistently challenges us to make creative use of our talents with diligence and hard work.

Gain all you can through gathered wisdom. Don't be like the foolish farmer who tried to decide on his own. We need wise counselors and financial advisors. We need the shared wisdom of the Christian community in which brothers and sisters in Christ can hold us accountable for the use of our resources and give us guidance in the hard choices we have to make.

> Without counsel, plans go
>   wrong,
>   but with many advisers they
>   succeed.
>   PROVERBS 15:22

Gain all you can without paying too high a price for it. Don't earn money at the expense of your health, your soul, or your

neighbor's well-being. Break the spell of *homo incurvatus in se.*
Contrary to what contemporary culture would have you believe,
your life is not defined by what you own. There is more to life
than the things you possess.

Gain all you can as you honor God. Trust the God who sus-
tains and cares for you. Allow the God revealed in Jesus Christ
to enter into your calculations of who you are and what to do
with what you have. Jesus promised that if we seek first his Kingdom, everything we need will be provided by the gracious God
who watches over his children with infinite care.

3. Save All You Can: The New Frugality

Having gained all you can, by honest wisdom and unwearied diligence, the second rule of Christian prudence is, "Save all you can." Do not throw it away in idle expenses, which is just the same as throwing it into the sea.

JOHN WESLEY, *"THE USE OF MONEY"*

Read Philippians 4:10-20.

DO YOU REMEMBER Stanley Johnson? He was the humorous character in a television commercial for a lending agency.

With a self-satisfied smile, Stanley introduced himself and his family, complete with two children and a dog. He showed us his four-bedroom home in a great neighborhood, his swimming pool, and his new car. With obvious pride, he let us know that he was a member of the local golf club. Grinning into the camera while he turned steaks on the backyard grill he asked, "How do I do it?" Still wearing a silly grin, he confided in the audience as he answered his own question: "I'm in debt up to my eyeballs. I can barely pay my finance charges." At the end of the commercial he pleaded, "Somebody help me."

About Stanley Johnson

I've never been able to forget Stanley Johnson. Since the first time I saw him, I've had three observations about his situation.

First, Stanley is not unusual. In fact, he's typical of far too many people in our contemporary culture. He represents the kind of financially irresponsible, socially acceptable, overreaching indebtedness that helped plunge the American economy into the ditch not long after his commercial appeared on our television screens.

When we met Stanley, American citizens were carrying an average of $9,000 in credit card debt. If they made the minimum payment each month, it would take thirty-one years to pay it off, and they would have paid $29,000 in interest. That's a $29,000 expense on $9,000 of value! More people declared bankruptcy in one year than graduated from college. One survey found that a surprising 25 percent of the American people said their best chance for funding retirement would be winning the lottery. Evidently, Stanley Johnson was a whole lot like many of us.

I heard about a husband who went through the ceiling when he saw the credit card bill. He asked his wife, "How many times do I have to tell you that it's economically irresponsible to spend money before we get it?" She replied, "I don't know about that. This way if you never get the money, at least you have something to show for it."

That's been the attitude of an instant-gratification, credit card-addicted, consumption-oriented culture. And that's what got Stanley Johnson—and many of us—into trouble. It's an irrational belief in "the myth of more," the illusion that all I need to be happy is more stuff. The result is that we bargain away our souls and mortgage our grandchildren's future so that we can have it all and have it now.

There's nothing new about the myth of more. The writer of Ecclesiastes warned, "Whoever loves money never has money enough; whoever loves wealth is never satisfied with his income" (Ecclesiastes 5:10 NIV).

My second observation is that Stanley's problems would not be solved by getting more money. His problem was not a shortage of money, but a shortage in management. It was not a lack of wealth, but a lack of wisdom. His problem was not his math, but his values. Besides dealing with the size of his debt, he needed a transformation in his heart. Behind his economic crisis he faced a spiritual one. It was the kind of crisis that might have created the opportunity for God to do a new thing in his life.

> Precious treasure remains in
> the house of the wise,
> but the fool devours it.
>
> PROVERBS 21:20

My third observation is that God really cares about Stanley Johnson and that the cure for his addiction is in the Bible and not in the bank.

Most people are surprised to discover that Jesus talked about money and possessions twice as much as he did about heaven and hell, five times as much as he talked about prayer, and that nearly half of Jesus' parables deal with how we manage money and possessions.

For many faithful people, it is equally surprising to learn that the vast majority of the Bible's references to money and possessions have less to do with fund-raising for the church or the welfare of the poor than they do with the spiritual health and well-being of the people who are possessed by their possessions.

Jesus' warnings to those who are rich offer both a word of judgment and a word of compassion. When he told his followers that it is easier for a camel to go through the eye of a needle than for a rich person to get into heaven, his primary concern was not the impact of a rich person's wealth on the welfare of the poor, but the impact of wealth on the spiritual well-being of the rich.

A prime example is the man who has become known as "the rich young ruler," a title that combines the stories found in Matthew 19:16-30 and Luke 18:18-30. In both accounts, the rich man turned and walked away, "grieving" (Matthew) and "sad" (Luke) because the things he possessed had taken possession of him.

The Bible says that God really cares about the way we manage our money or, conversely, the way our money manages us.

God's plan for the management of our money is designed to help each of us experience a fuller, freer, more abundant life.

That was Wesley's concern as well. His "plain rules" on the use of money were designed to guide faithful Christian people in developing patterns of personal and financial discipline that would enable them to experience the fullness of life that God intends for every one of his children. In fact, Wesley's challenge to "save all you can" is precisely the help that Stanley Johnson needed.

How Not to Save

I read the story of a woman in Tel Aviv who attempted to perform a "random act of kindness" for her mother. She decided to surprise the elderly woman with a new mattress. She brought the new mattress to her mother's home and threw out the old one without telling her. We can only imagine the look of surprise on the daughter's face when she learned that her mother had hidden her life savings of one million dollars inside the old mattress. No wonder it was lumpy!

When the daughter realized her mistake, she ran to the curb to retrieve the mattress, only to discover that the garbage trucks had already made their rounds. Newspapers around the world carried the picture of the woman searching through a mountain of refuse at the local dump site. The dump manager, surely understating the truth when he said the woman appeared to be "totally desperate," acknowledged that the mattress would be nearly impossible to find in the 2,500 tons of rubbish that arrived every day.[1] When Wesley told his followers to "save all you can," we can be sure that stuffing cash in a mattress was not what he had in mind! He was talking about more than hoarding money in a savings account. He was calling his followers to a pattern of living that is grounded in a person's relationship with God and that expresses itself in the whole of a person's life.

"Having gained all you can by honest wisdom and unwearied

diligence," Wesley wrote, "the second rule of Christian prudence is, 'Save all you can.' Do not throw it away in idle expenses, which is just the same as throwing it into the sea."

> Wealth hastily gotten will
> dwindle,
> but those who gather little by
> little will increase it.
> PROVERBS 13:11

Waste Not, Want Not

The key word for Wesley in this passage of the sermon is *waste*. He begins by warning us not to waste our money "in gratifying the desires of the flesh...particularly, in enlarging the pleasure of tasting."

Wesley calls us not only to avoid gluttony and drunkenness, but to stay away from "an elegant epicurism [sic], which does not immediately disorder the stomach...and yet cannot be maintained without considerable expense." In no uncertain terms, he says we should "despise delicacy and variety, and be content with what plain nature requires."

There's practical wisdom in Wesley's warning that includes but goes beyond the financial considerations. A report from the Trust for America's Health found that in 2009, obesity rates among adults rose in twenty-three states and did not decline in any. In three states, more than 30 percent of the adult population was unhealthily obese.[2] Spend a few minutes observing the girth of people in any large crowd and you will quickly come to the conclusion that the American people are eating themselves to death.

The Christian community carries a special responsibility in this area of stewardship. In the chapter on gluttony in my book *Strength for the Broken Places*, I shared the results of a study by Ken Ferraro, a sociologist at Purdue University, who tracked the connections between religion and body weight. He observed that

"America is becoming known as a nation of gluttony and obesity and churches are a feeding ground for the problem." He said that while churches historically have raised concern about the most injurious behaviors, such as smoking and irresponsible use of alcohol, "overeating is not considered a great sin—it has become the accepted vice."[3]

John Wesley would not have been surprised by Ferraro's findings. Given the economic impact of the "accepted vice" of our unhealthy eating habits, his warning about wasting money on unhealthful food has a prophetic ring.

Besides warning us about our eating habits, Wesley goes on to challenge us not to waste money "in gratifying the desire of the eye."

In a time when some of his followers were becoming more prosperous, Wesley warned them about wasting money on "superfluous or expensive apparel or needless ornaments...in curiously adorning your houses; in superfluous or expensive furniture...in elegant rather than useful gardens."

There's practical wisdom for us there, too. We are constantly bombarded with advertisements that urge us to buy more and more expensive and totally unnecessary stuff. As a result, many people end up owing more money on mortgages than their homes are worth or carrying unsustainable credit card debt, because they bought more superfluous stuff than they could ever afford. That's what got Stanley Johnson into such a mess. Wesley's call for a more modest lifestyle sounds wiser every day.

In his sermon, Wesley continues by warning us not to waste our money "to gain the admiration or praise of men."

Wesley saw a connection between his previous warnings and this one. He said that people are "expensive in diet, or apparel, or furniture, not barely to please their appetite, or to gratify their eye...but their vanity too." He told his followers that they should not "buy their applause so dear. Rather be content with the honour that cometh from God."

Today we would call that "keeping up with the Joneses."

Whatever term we use, Wesley challenges us not to waste money trying to impress other people. He calls us to find identity in our relationship with God rather than in our relationship with our possessions; to seek the honor of God rather than the honor that comes from owning the largest house on the block.

Playwright Tennessee Williams expressed the wisdom of Scripture in his play *Cat on a Hot Tin Roof* when he had Big Daddy say, "The human animal is a beast that dies and if he's got money he buys and buys and buys and I think the reason he buys everything he can buy is that in the back of his mind he has the crazy hope that one of his purchases will be life everlasting! Which it never can be."[4]

> When you grab all you can get, that's what happens:
> the more you get, the less you are.
> PROVERBS 1:19 *THE MESSAGE*

Fighting the Consumption Addiction

Beneath Wesley's specific warnings was his awareness that consumption becomes addictive. "Daily experience shows," he wrote, "the more they are indulged, they increase the more."

There's a name for this addiction: shopoholism. A 2006 study at Stanford University determined that compulsive overspending or "overshopping" is a disorder that affects approximately 17,000,000 people, roughly 6 percent of the United States population. It's the addiction of going to the mall not to buy something we need, but to see what we can buy.

The Public Health Department at Indiana University provides a Web site on "How to Manage Compulsive Shopping and Spending Addiction." What caught my attention was the red-letter notice at the top of the page: "Note: I am no longer able to answer questions about shopping addiction due to large number of hits on this site."[5] There are evidently a lot of folk out there who know that they are addicted!

Teach Your Children Well

Because Wesley knew the addictive power of consumerism, he turned his attention to the responsibility of parents for the welfare of their children. He sounds downright countercultural when he tells parents not to "throw away money upon your children" by giving them everything they think they want.

Magazine editor Skye Jethani, in his article "Stranded in Neverland," provides a vivid image of the situation in which many of us find ourselves. He describes a consumer economy that attempts to create a "culture of immaturity and overindulgence.... Although lack of self-control has always plagued humanity, for the first time in history an economic system has been created that relies on it."[6]

As both a father and pastor, I never cease to be amazed at the number of young adults who say that their parents never taught them how to manage money. Even more shocking are the number of parents who think they are expressing love for their children by giving them everything the children think they want. These parents seem unaware that they are feeding their children the addictive drug of consumerism and creating a new generation of shopoholics.

It is part of our duty as Christian parents to model the responsible use of money and to teach our children that they don't necessarily need everything the culture conditions them to want.

Growing up in a small town in western Pennsylvania, I must have been ten or twelve years old when I started delivering *The Pittsburgh Press* on my bicycle. I went to the bank with my parents to open a checking account in my name, and I remember sitting with them around the dining room table to learn how to balance my checkbook. That's when they taught me that the first 10 percent of my earnings, called a tithe, belongs to God. They taught me that part of what I earned needed to go into savings, in the form of a U.S. Savings Bond. And they taught me that the rest was mine to spend wisely and well.

Today we call the lesson my parents taught me the "10-10-80 Plan": 10 percent for God, 10 percent for the future, and 80 percent to live on. We didn't have a nifty formula for it back then, but it was the way my parents taught me to manage my money. It's the way we taught our daughters to manage their money, too. It represents the countercultural wisdom that the Bible provides to help us manage our money.

> The borrower is the slave
> of the lender.
> PROVERBS 22:7

While his attention was focused on children, John Wesley turned to the matter of inheritance. He unraveled the ordinary patterns of inheritance when he declared, "How amazing then is the infatuation of those parents who think they can never leave their children enough!"

Warren Buffet had a classic answer to the question of how much a rich person should leave the kids: "enough to do anything but not enough to do nothing." John Wesley put a spiritual spin on the same principle when he wrote, "Give each what would keep him above want, and bestow all the rest in such a manner as would be most for the glory of God."

A New Frugality

The opposite of waste is frugality. Contrary to some impressions, the word *frugal* does not mean cheap or stingy. It comes from a Latin root for "useful" or "temperate." It means "without waste." A frugal person knows how to use everything wisely and well.

I discovered a contemporary version of Wesley's sermon in a *Time* magazine cover article titled "The New Frugality." The writer said that in the face of economic hardship, Boomers such as me are "channeling our grandparents, who were taught, like a mantra, to use it up, wear it out, make it do, do without." The writer sounded like one of Wesley's preachers when he wrote:

> As we pick through the economic rubble, we may find that our riches have buried our treasures. Money does not buy happiness; Scripture asserts this, research confirms it. Once you reach the median level of income, roughly $50,000 a year, wealth and contentment go their separate ways, and studies find that a millionaire is no more likely to be happy than someone earning one-twentieth as much.... A consumer culture invites us to want more than we can ever have; a culture of thrift invites us to be grateful for whatever we can get.[7]

On her blog for women, Lisa Earle McLeod declared frugality to be "the new cool" when she wrote, "The recession is now official—my teenager no longer shops at Abercrombie & Fitch." She went on to say:

> By bankrupting our economy with their greed and corruption, the money men of Wall Street have accomplished what Main Street moms have been trying to do for decades. They've shown our kids that consumption does not equate to happiness, and they're forcing the next generation to become more prudent with their money.... It's the new trend, pass it along."[8]

Along the way we rediscover wisdom that the biblical writers have always known: frugality can lead to contentment. In studying the changes resulting from the economic meltdown in the American economy, sociologist Michael Maniates found that "people are coming to realize they can live with less and their lives are richer for it."[9]

> All the days of the poor are
> hard,
>   but a cheerful heart has a
>   continual feast.
>   PROVERBS 15:15

Learning Contentment

Paul's letter to the Philippians is a case in point. Paul was in prison, probably in Rome. He was completely dependent for his survival on the generosity of his friends. He wrote the letter to thank the folks in Philippi for the gift of support they had sent. Along with his gratitude, he wanted to assure them that he was okay, regardless of his circumstances. He wrote, "I have learned to be content with whatever I have."

Fellow pastor Matt Horan said that he is considering purchasing T-shirts showing those words of Paul for his young daughters to wear when they go to the mall. It's not a bad idea! Here is Paul's witness:

> I have learned to be content with whatever I have. I know what it is to have little, and I know what it is to have plenty. In any and all circumstances I have learned the secret of being well-fed and of going hungry, of having plenty and of being in need. I can do all things through him who strengthens me.
>
> PHILIPPIANS 4:11-13

Paul concluded the chapter with his bold statement that "my God will fully satisfy every need of yours according to his riches in glory in Christ Jesus" (v. 19).

The letter to the Hebrews reinforced Paul's words: "Keep your lives free from the love of money, and be content with what you have; for [God] has said, "I will never leave you or forsake you" (Hebrews 13:5).

The apostle described an inner contentment that is not dependent on external resources. It's the calm center that is formed in our hearts when we begin to sort out the difference between what we want and what we need. It's a contentment that grows out of a soul-level confidence in the goodness and faithfulness of God.

The purpose of Wesley's instruction to save all we can was not for the sake of amassing a huge savings account or investment fund. The goal of this spiritual discipline was contentment; the assurance that we can face whatever comes, through the power of Christ at work within us.

> Those who trust in their riches
>   will wither,
>   but the righteous will flourish
>   like green leaves.
>
> PROVERBS 11:28

In the spirit of Wesley's practical advice, here is my own home-grown version of how to "save all you can."

Face the facts. Some of us need to take a ruthless inventory of what we earn and what we spend. The pattern in American culture has been to live beyond our means by habitually spending more than we earn. The new frugality begins when we see exactly how much money is coming in compared with how much is going out. The surprise often comes in discovering exactly where the money is going. When many folks take a thorough inventory of their income and expenses, they are surprised by how much they have, how much they spend, and how they spend it.

Ask for help. Jesus told the story of a foolish builder who didn't calculate the cost of construction and was unable to finish his project (Luke 14:28–30). Particularly in difficult economic times, the Stanley Johnson in each of us needs a competent financial advisor to help us make wise and stable investments.

We also need the accountability of trusted brothers or sisters in the community of faith. Many churches are helping their people make responsible financial decisions by using Dave Ramsey's *Financial Peace University* or Willow Creek's *Good Sense* program.

Set clear priorities for spending. Begin with the essentials: housing, food, clothing, transportation. Be absolutely ruthless in sorting out what is essential from the things you can live without. Know the true value of everything you purchase. The writer of Proverbs gives us the model of the wise woman who "considers a field and buys it. . . . She perceives that her merchandise is profitable" (Proverbs 31:16-18).

Live below your income. Look for ways to reduce your expenditures to fit within your income. Did Stanley Johnson really need the big house, the new car, and the golf club membership? I saw a news story about the way the economic crisis has led to an increase in the use of grocery store coupons, the purchase of less-expensive store brands, and the way wise shoppers are looking for "two-for-one" food items.

Do plastic surgery. Develop a plan to get rid of credit card debt. If you are unable to pay off the credit card balance every month, cut up the cards and practice the discipline of not buying anything unless you can pay for it with cash.

Break the shopoholic addiction. Avoid going to the mall as a way of entertainment or recreation. Only go shopping when you have made a careful decision about what you intend to purchase. Buy it and get out of the mall before you are tempted to purchase unnecessary stuff.

Eric Dykstra offered his Minnesota congregation a "100 Thing Challenge" in which he encouraged them to reduce their possession to 100 or fewer items. He said the purpose was "to break the hold of materialism." In the process, he reduced his wardrobe from five suits to one and from a dozen ties to two. He reported: "It was very freeing."[10]

Be content with what you have. Learn the lesson that contentment cannot be purchased. It is more a matter of the soul than of the bank account. A 2009 MetLife study of the American dream found that 47 percent of consumers say that they already have everything they need, an increase of 37 percent in three years.[11]

Trust God. Use the economic crisis as motivation to move into a deeper relationship of trust in God, in the assurance that you can do all things through the One who strengthens you.

Hope for Stanley Johnson

We began this chapter with the fictional story of Stanley Johnson. Let me close with the true story of a man who discovered the contentment that comes in ordering our financial lives around our faith in Christ.

My friend's life was a mess. He was in the middle of a painful divorce. He had left a comfortable home in the suburbs and moved into a one-bedroom apartment. His furniture was odds and ends that friends had given him. He was alone. His career had hit the rocks. He was broke. He said it was the lowest point of his life.

One day he went for a long run to see if it would make him feel better. Halfway along his route, the clouds opened up and the rain came down in buckets. He thought to himself, "How bad can it get?" That's when he started to pray. He said, "Lord, I've really made a mess of things. It's about time I turn my life over to you." And he did, right then and there. Slogging through the rain, in a simple act of faith, he surrendered the control of his life to Jesus Christ.

Somewhere in his past, he had heard that when people get serious about giving their lives to Christ, a tangible expression of that commitment is tithing, giving the first 10 percent of our income to God's work in the world as an act of trust in God's ability to provide for our needs. He was over thirty thousand dollars in debt and had a grand total of thirty dollars in his checkbook. He said it was tough to write that first check for 10 percent, but he figured, "What have I got to lose?" and did it.

That's when God began to turn his life around. Over time, step by painful step, the Spirit led him out of his depression and into a new life. He got involved in the church. He joined a Bible study group that has nurtured and strengthened his faith. He went to work to get his financial house in order. In time, he met a woman who shares his commitment to Christ. He discovered his spiritual gifts and has found a way God can use his experience to serve others. Today, he's one of the most joyful people I know. Here's the way he described what God did in his life:

Six months after I started tithing, I was debt-free. Miraculous things happened. I got a new job for a company that decided to open a regional office. It wasn't much, but I was employee number-one down here. Today we have eighty-six employees and are the most profitable office in the company. I was on the verge of departing the military reserves because I just was lost—without sense of purpose or focus. I refocused and am now a colonel in the reserves. My predivorce savings was a twelfth of what we have in the bank today.

In my mind, all this has happened because for the last five years, I have been giving between 10 and 15 percent of my earnings to God. I do it no matter what other bills look like. I'm not quite sure how we do that but we keep doing it. The more we give, the more we have.

A skeptic could say that all this might have happened even if he had not decided to trust God with his tithe, but you'll never convince my friend of that.

I didn't start to tithe to see how God would bless me. I did it because I felt I needed to. It wasn't to receive financial gain. The blessings we have received are amazing and beyond description. I think it's God's way of telling us that perhaps we are on the right track. I still have a long way to go but I mean to keep going!

Imagine the difference it would make to Stanley Johnson if he could learn that kind of connection between his faith and his finances. Just imagine the difference it could make for you!

4. Give All You Can: A New Generosity

What way then ... can we take that our money may not sink us to the nethermost hell? There is one way, and there is no other under heaven. If those who "gain all they can" and "save all they can" will likewise "give all they can," then the more they gain the more they will grow in grace, and the more treasure they will lay up in heaven.

JOHN WESLEY, "THE USE OF MONEY"

Read: 1 Timothy 6:6-21.

THE TEAM THAT comes up with creative ways to communicate the theme of our worship services at Hyde Park United Methodist Church found a video spoof on those television commercials that promise a cure for everything from restless leg syndrome to male sexual dysfunction.

The commercial begins with a close-up shot of a man who looks into the camera with the sincerity of a person who is sharing the most intimate secret of his life. He tells us that he is afflicted with "closed-fist syndrome (CFS)," a recognized medical condition defined as "the overwhelming urge to hold onto cash at all costs." As a result, the man is unable to unclench his fists, which are grasping handfuls of dollar bills. The syndrome gets him into some difficult situations, such as trying to brush his teeth, pay for a cup of coffee at the drive-through window, or release any of his dollars as the offering plate passes by.

Help comes when the man's doctor recommends a drug called Generis (fingerpryus HCL). This drug relieves the CFS symptoms that keep people from giving, releasing them to share the dollars in their hands with others. The commercial ends with a comical version of the typical drug warnings. I expected a warning that if the effects of Generis last more than four hours, they might last a lifetime.

Healing for CFS

There seems to be a lot of CFS going around these days. It's as prevalent as the common cold, particularly in precarious economic times. The condition is often brought on by fear. In his *Financial Peace University*, Dave Ramsey identifies fear as a major contributing factor to the recent economic crisis. Adam Hamilton points to "overactive fear mechanisms" as one of the issues every faithful person needs to confront in order to find the joy of simplicity and generosity. Hamilton says that "living in fear means not really living at all."[1]

> Those who listen to me will be secure
> and will live at ease, without dread of disaster.
> PROVERBS 1:33

In 1791, John Wesley published his book *Primitive Physick: Or an Easy and Natural Method of Curing Most Diseases*. It included, in alphabetical order, Wesley's cures for everything from apoplexy to warts. For baldness he prescribed rubbing the head with an onion, then rubbing it with honey, but he did not report on the effectiveness of this treatment. Though Wesley did not include closed-fist syndrome in his list of ailments, he did provide the cure for it as part of "three plain rules" in his sermon "The Use of Money."

Wesley clearly intended for the prescription to be taken progressively, one treatment building on the previous one, leading toward a healthy relationship between our faith and our finances. We can hear the urgency in his voice when he declared:

> Let not any man imagine that he has done anything, barely by going thus far, by "gaining and saving all he can," if he were to stop here. All this is nothing, if a man go not forward, if he does

not point all this at a farther end. Nor, indeed, can a man properly be said to save anything, if he only lays it up. You may as well throw your money into the sea, as bury it in the earth.... Not to use, is effectually to throw it away. Therefore...add the Third rule to the two preceding. Having, First, gained all you can, and, Secondly saved all you can, Then "give all you can."[2]

I couldn't find evidence of it in Wesley's journal, but my guess is that when he came to this point in the sermon, someone in the crowd must have said, "I knew it! Here comes the 'bait and switch.' I knew that sooner or later this would end up being a fund-raising sermon for the Methodists!"

Wesley was never hesitant about asking for money to support his movement. In fact, he could really pour it on, particularly when he was raising money to meet the needs of the poor. But that wasn't the purpose of this particular sermon.

In this case, the urgency behind Wesley's sermon was his passionate desire to lead people into a healthier, more productive, more positive life by providing practical wisdom on the relationship between their faith and their finances. Wesley's rules are not about fund-raising for the church; they are about becoming more like Christ. They are about practicing the spiritual discipline of generosity so that we become generous people whose lives are shaped in the likeness of an extravagantly generous God.

> Those who despise their
>   neighbors are sinners,
>   but happy are those who are
>   kind to the poor.
>   PROVERBS 14:21

Created to Give but Tempted to Keep

When our worship planning team wrestled with how John Wesley's words might speak to our congregation today, here were some of the themes that emerged from our conversation.

- We are created to give, but we are tempted to keep.
- The more we have, the larger our temptation to hoard.
- If we want to grow into a Christ-centered life, we need to learn the spiritual discipline of generosity.
- How can we find the balance between frugality and giving; security and generosity?
- When is enough enough?
- We need a fresh, positive, and joyful vision of the way our generosity becomes a part of God's transformation of the world.
- We need to be reminded that generosity is good for the heart and soul.
- For followers of Christ, giving is not an incidental activity, but an essential spiritual discipline that moves us toward a Christ-centered life.

Those were the kinds of concerns that motivated Wesley. They are also the concerns that motivated Paul in his letter to Timothy. The apostle wrote that are the folks for whom the primary motivating desire in life is to get rich. In his sermon on this text, "The Danger of Riches," Wesley described them as people who "aim at and endeavour after, not only so much worldly substance as will procure them the necessaries and conveniences of life, but more than this, whether to lay it up, or lay it out in superfluities...all who *possess* more of this world's goods than they use according to the will of the Donor: I should rather say, of the Proprietor; for He only *lends* them to us as Stewards; reserving the *property* of them to himself."[3]

In his letter to Timothy, Paul warned that people whose lives are organized around the desire to get rich "fall into temptation." (Wesley's phrasing was "They fall plump down into it.") Paul said these people are easily "trapped by many senseless and harmful desires.... In their eagerness to be rich they have wandered away from the faith and pierced themselves with many pains" (1 Timothy 6:9-10).

Eugene Peterson captured the urgency of Paul's warning in his paraphrase of Paul's words:

> But if it's only money these leaders are after, they'll self-destruct in no time. Lust for money brings trouble and nothing but trouble. Going down that path, some lose their footing in the faith completely and live to regret it bitterly ever after.
>
> 1 TIMOTHY 6:9-10, *THE MESSAGE*

When John Wesley preached on this text, he asked some tough questions: "Who believes that? Who is deeply convinced of it? Who preaches this strange doctrine? Who has the courage to declare so unfashionable a truth?"[4]

Paul's warning about what happens to people whose lives are driven by a desire to get rich is just as "unfashionable a truth" today as it was in the eighteenth century. It's true not because it is in the Bible; it's in the Bible because it is true. It proves itself to be true in every age. We do not break this truth so much as we break ourselves upon it.

In the summer of 2009, the daily headlines provided empirical evidence of the timeless truth of the apostle's words. That's when Bernard Madoff was sentenced to 150 years in prison for pulling off the most gigantic financial fraud in U.S. history. The destruction of his own life and the damaged lives that were left in his wake will go down in history as a dramatic witness of the way the desire to get rich at all costs inevitably results in loss and pain.

> Better is a little with
> righteousness
> than large income with
> injustice.
>
> PROVERBS 16:8

The Madoff scandal was the largest and most dramatic symptom of the insidious infection of uninhibited greed that swept through the American financial system. But on a much smaller scale, too many people were far too willing to do whatever they could to satisfy their insatiable desire to get rich. The mood of the time was to gain all you can, in every way you can, as fast as you can, with as little restraint as you can. As long as everyone was getting rich—or thought they were getting rich—the hot air kept filling the economic balloon until it finally blew up in our faces.

Life That Is Really Life

Paul said there is an alternative to a life driven by the desire to get rich. He called the followers of Christ to a radically different way of living. It's the biblical cure for "closed-fist syndrome."

The apostle urged the people of God to "shun all this" and to pursue the things of God that last forever: righteousness, godliness, faith, love, endurance, gentleness. He encouraged Timothy to "take hold of the eternal life" to which we are called in Christ. He challenged Timothy to instruct those who have wealth to be "rich in good works...so that they may take hold of the life that really is life." Here is Eugene Peterson's paraphrase:

> Tell those rich in this world's wealth to quit being so full of themselves and so obsessed with money.... Tell them to go after God, who piles on all the riches we could ever manage—to do good, to be rich in helping others, to be extravagantly generous. If they do that, they'll build a treasury that will last, gaining life that is truly life.
>
> 1 TIMOTHY 6:17-19, *THE MESSAGE*

Paul's call to extravagant generosity, along with Wesley's challenge to give all we can, is about more than just writing an occasional check to our favorite charity on the basis of some momentary, emotional appeal. It defines a total reorientation of our financial life around our commitment to Christ. It's about practicing generosity as a spiritual discipline by which we become more like Jesus. It's a call to economic practices by which we experience "the life that really is life."

It All Belongs to God

Wesley begins the final section of his sermon "The Use of Money" by reminding us who God is and who we are. He names God as "the Possessor of heaven and earth (who) brought you into being, and placed you in this world." That's where biblical faith always begins. The foundational affirmation of Scripture is expressed in Psalm 24:

> The earth is the LORD's and all
>   that is in it,
>   the world and those who live
>   in it;
> for he has founded it on the
>   seas,
>   and established it on the
>   rivers.
> PSALM 24:1-2

The psalmist says that this earth and those within it belong to God by right of creation. The writer of the epistle of James reaffirms that conviction by saying that every good gift comes from God (James 1:17). Throughout the New Testament, the understanding is that everything we have belongs to God because of God's extravagant act of generosity and grace in the life, death, and resurrection of Jesus Christ.

Paul asked and then answered his own rhetorical question to the Corinthians: "Do you not know that your body is a temple of the Holy Spirit within you, which you have from God, and that you are not your own? For you were bought with a price; therefore glorify God in your body" (1 Corinthians 6:19-20).

At the cross, the relentless love and undeserved grace of God "bought back" a rebellious world that had rejected God's ownership of it. God is the possessor of heaven and earth and all that is within it, first by right of creation, and second by right of redemption. It all belongs to God.

John Wesley's brother Charles celebrated God's ownership of all that we have and are when he wrote:

> Let him to whom we now belong
> His sovereign right assert,
> And take up every thankful song,
> And every loving heart.
>
> He justly claims us for his own,
> Who bought us with a price;
> The Christian lives to Christ alone,
> To Christ alone he dies.
>
> Our souls and bodies we resign;
> With joy we render thee
> Our all, no longer ours, but thine
> To all eternity.[5]

Remember Who You Are

Once we get it through our heads who God is and what God has done, we discover a very different perspective on who we are. Wesley said, "He placed you here not as a proprietor, but as a steward." We are stewards; temporary, short-term managers of property that belongs to God.

Wesley reminds us that God entrusted everything we have into our hands "for a season . . . goods of various kinds . . . all that you enjoy. Such is your soul and your body, not your own, but God's. And so is your substance in particular." As temporary stewards or managers of property that belongs to God, we are called to "employ it for him, in such as manner that it may be acceptable through Christ Jesus."

Across our years in ministry, my family has been blessed by

the generosity of friends who have lent us their vacation homes for rest and renewal. In stressful times, I often take an imaginary journey back to those homes: a historic lodge in the Rocky Mountains of Colorado, a condominium on the Atlantic coast, a beach house on the Gulf of Mexico, a creekside cabin in the Smoky Mountains of North Carolina. In each place, we were made to feel welcome and at home. Everything within the house was available for our use. But we were always aware that the house and everything in it belonged to someone else.

The owners lent it to us for a time with the intention that we would use and enjoy it the way they did, thereby fulfilling the owners' original intention in building it. It did not belong to us. After a time in our hands, the keys would be returned to their rightful owner. We felt a responsibility to use and care for the place in ways that reflected our gratitude to the owner. We were stewards for a time of things that belonged to someone else. Wesley says the same thing about our bodies and souls.

The point is that when we give all we can, we are not giving God something that belongs to us. When we give, we are using what belongs to God in ways that honor its owner. Our generosity becomes a finite, human expression of the infinite generosity of God.

> A generous person will be
>   enriched,
> and one who gives water will
>   get water.
>   PROVERBS 11:25

Paul underscores the point by reminding us that we brought nothing into this world and we will take nothing from it (1 Timothy 6:7). He probably learned that from the Old Testament story of Job, who said, "Naked I came from my mother's womb, and naked shall I return there; the LORD gave, and the LORD has taken away; blessed be the name of the LORD" (Job 1:21).

John Ortberg created a vivid image of this biblical principle in the title of his book, when he described our lives as a game of Monopoly in which, *When the Game Is Over, It All Goes Back in the Box.*[6]

In 1979, I was in worship at the Riverside Church of New York on the Sunday after the church hosted the funeral for Nelson Rockefeller. Aside from Rockefeller's political life as a former Vice President of the United States and Governor of New York, he was a member of the church, which had been built and endowed by his grandfather, John D. Rockefeller, Sr. I've never been able to forget the honesty with which the pastor, William Sloane Coffin, Jr., told the congregation that Rockefeller's death reminded him that "this is God's world. At best, we are guests. Even the Rockefellers are guests in this world."[7]

The sudden death of Michael Jackson in 2009 created a global communications phenomenon, and people around the globe watched every detail of the story. It would be difficult to find a more powerful witness to the truth of Job's words than the televised images as the body of the "King of Pop," who had amassed and spent wealth beyond any ordinary person's comprehension, was transported to the Los Angeles coroner's office wrapped in a plain white sheet. That's the way we all come into this world; that's the way we all leave it. In between, we are temporary managers of property that belongs to God.

> A life devoted to things is a dead life, a stump;
> A God-shaped life is a flourishing tree.
> PROVERBS 11:28, *THE MESSAGE*

Wesley's Surprise

With this biblical understanding of who God is and who we are, Wesley moves to the specific ways in which we practice faithful stewardship of the money that God entrusts into our hands. And this is where he surprised me.

I expected him to begin with tithing, the biblical discipline of giving the first 10 percent of all that we earn back to God for God's work in this world. I was taught and continue to teach the biblical principle of putting God first in our lives by giving our "first fruits" as an act of spiritual and financial discipline. But that's not where Wesley begins. He begins with our own needs and builds concentric circles that reach out from us.

> If you desire to be a faithful and a wise steward.... First, provide things needful for yourself; food to eat, raiment to put on, whatever nature moderately requires for preserving the body in health and strength.[8]

The operative phrases are "things needful" and "whatever nature moderately requires." We learned in the previous chapter what Wesley thought about extravagant food, designer-label clothing, expensive jewelry, and elaborate home décor. He consistently called his followers to practice modesty and moderation, and he modeled it himself. When proceeds began to roll in from his writings, for example, Wesley determined how much he needed in order to live and gave the rest away. His actions are yet another reminder that the life of discipleship always involves sorting out what we want from what we need. But even so, he begins with our needs in the center circle.

In the next concentric circle, Wesley tells us to "provide these for your wife, your children . . . or any others who pertain to your household." (My wife was happy to hear that!) Finally, in the third concentric circle, he challenges us to reach out to the needs of others.

> If when this is done there be an overplus left, then "do good to them that are of the household of faith." If there be an overplus still, "as you have opportunity, do good unto all men." In so doing, you give all you can; nay, in a sound sense, all you have: For all that is laid out in this manner is really given to God. You "render unto God the things that are God's," not only by what you give to the poor, but also by that which you expend in providing things needful for yourself and your household.[9]

My surprise that Wesley puts my needs in the first circle was tempered by the questions he challenges us to ask every time we prepare to spend our money—or rather, the money that Wesley describes as "your Lord's goods which he has for the present lodged in your hands, but with the right of resuming whenever it pleases him." When listing the questions, Wesley promises, "You will seldom need anything more to remove any doubt which arises on this head; but by this four-fold consideration you will receive clear light as to the way wherein you should go." Here are the four questions:

1. In expending this, am I acting according to my character? Am I acting herein, not as a proprietor, but as a steward of my Lord's goods?
2. Am I doing this in obedience to his Word? In what Scripture does he require me so to do?
3. Can I offer up this action, this expense, as a sacrifice to God through Jesus Christ?
4. Have I reason to believe that for this very work I shall have a reward at the resurrection of the just?[10]

How would you like to go through that list of questions every time you head off to the mall?

If the four questions aren't challenging enough, he tells us to offer this prayer to "the Searcher of hearts" before we make any purchase. I've adapted his eighteenth-century language to make it a little clearer for us.

Lord, you see I am going to expend this sum on that food, apparel, furniture. I do this with a single eye as a steward of your goods, expending this portion of them in ways that are consistent with the design you had in mind when you entrusted them to me. I do this in obedience to you. Let this purchase be a holy sacrifice, acceptable through Jesus Christ! And give me a witness in myself that for this labor of love I shall receive a reward when you judge everyone according to their works.[11]

Wesley concludes that if, after this kind of self-examination and prayer, our conscience bears witness that our proposed expenditure is consistent with the will of God, then we will know it is right and good and we can go ahead and enjoy it as a way of giving all that we have and all that we are to God.

> Those who are generous are
> blessed,
> for they share their bread with
> the poor.
> PROVERBS 22:9

It's important to remember that Wesley's guidelines for spending, as severe as they might seem, were presented in the context of his rule, "Give all you can." What he was talking about, in other words, was the spiritual discipline of generosity. In the spirit of John Wesley, then, here are a few of my own ideas about generosity.

Generosity is essential. Generosity is not optional for Christian people. It is not the exclusive practice of the saints; it is the basic practice of every disciple. Giving all we can is a nonnegotiable practice of the Christ-centered life, because it shapes our lives around the extravagant generosity of God.

Paul was instructing the Corinthians on their use of money when he wrote, "You know the generous act of our Lord Jesus Christ, that though he was rich, yet for your sakes he became poor, so that by his poverty you might become rich" (2 Corinthians 8:9). We are called to practice generosity because God has been so extravagantly generous to us in Christ.

The Bible says that real life, real joy, and real abundance are found, not in how much I get, but in how much I give. For Christ-followers, giving is a defiant act of rebellion against the insatiable power of greed. It's the countercultural behavior by which we refuse to let the world squeeze us into its mold and in which we are transformed into the mindset of the Christ who gave himself for us (see Romans 12:1-2).

In the Broadway show *Hello, Dolly*, the lead character declares, "Money is like manure; it's not worth a thing unless it's spread around encouraging things to grow." I discovered that Dolly got that from Frances Bacon, the seventeenth-century Lord Chancellor of England, who said, "Money is like manure, of very little use except it be spread."[12]

After three decades in pastoral ministry, I can honestly say that I have never known a person who moved deeply into a Christ-centered life who did not become more generous in their giving along the way. I've known many who tried, but none who succeeded in growing closer to Christ without learning to give.

> The wicked borrow, and do not
>   pay back,
>   but the righteous are generous
>   and keep giving.
>   PSALM 37:21

Generosity is intentional. It doesn't just happen. We don't become generous unless we plan for it. I know that if I waited to give until after I had provided for everything else, there would be no money left to give. We must plan to be generous. It is an intentional discipline of the Christian life.

That's the difference between charitable giving and Christian stewardship. Charitable giving is a good thing, but it generally comes from the leftovers of our lives and is usually motivated by a specific need or request. Christian stewardship is a disciplined pattern of giving that is motivated by our identity as a child of God and becomes a consistent part of the way we live.

> The plans of the diligent lead
>   surely to abundance,
>   but everyone who is hasty
>   comes only to want.
>   PROVERBS 21:5

This is where the spiritual discipline of tithing comes in. The biblical practice of setting aside the first 10 percent of our income for God's work in the world enables us to build consistent generosity into our personal or family budget. It's as intentional as paying the mortgage or electric bill. When I include my tithe in the budget, it becomes the foundation beneath which my generosity does not fall. I have a friend who says that tithing is a great place for generosity to begin, but it is a terrible place for generosity to end.

This is also an opportunity to say that Christian generosity ought to be just as intentional in death as it is in life. It is a Christian responsibility to prepare a will or estate plan as part of our financial stewardship.

A preacher friend told me about a woman who came into his office with a large donation to the church. In expressing his gratitude he said, "Well, I guess you can't take it with you." Quick as a wink she shot back, "I would if I could!"

But we can't. Shrouds don't have pockets, and hearses don't pull U-Haul trailers. Including God's work in my will is a form of intentional generosity ensuring that what I've believed in life will continue beyond my death.

A woman in her fifties died unexpectedly of a heart attack. When the estate was settled, we discovered that she had named the church as the beneficiary of a life insurance policy. It enabled her to provide a gift in death that was significantly larger than she probably would have been able to give in life, a gift that would ensure that the ministry of the church she so deeply loved would continue into the future.

Generosity is joyful. Another lesson I've learned from pastoral experience is that generous people are happy people and stingy people are grouches. When Paul said, "God loves a cheerful giver," he was acknowledging that we experience the joy at the heart of God when we practice generosity.

There is great joy in knowing that by our giving, we share in the way God is blessing others. There is great joy in seeing the way our generosity touches the life of this world with the love and grace of God. There is great joy in discovering that through our generosity, we participate in God's transformation of our world into some small part of the Kingdom of God. Through our generosity, we discover "the life that really is life."

> The world of the generous gets larger and larger;
> The world of the stingy gets smaller and smaller.
> The one who blesses others is abundantly blessed;
> Those who help others are helped.
> PROVERBS 11:24-27 *THE MESSAGE*

* * *

So, there they are: three plain rules with which John Wesley defined "Christian prudence so far as it relates to the use of that great talent, money." Wesley summarized his sermon by saying, "Gain all you can, without hurting either yourself or your neighbour... save all you can, by cutting off every expense which serves only to indulge foolish desire... and then, give all you can...that you may give a good account of your stewardship...in that day when the Lord cometh with all his saints."[13]

Never one to leave people without a call to response, Wesley concluded with this challenge:

> I entreat you, in the name of the Lord Jesus, act up to the dignity of your calling! No more sloth!...No more waste!...No more covetousness!...employ whatever God has entrusted you with, in doing good, all possible good, in every possible kind and degree, to the household of faith, to all men!...Give all ye have, as well as all ye are...to him who withheld not from you his only Son: So...that ye may attain eternal life![14]

We began this exploration of Wesley's rules by asking what it might take for us to make radical changes in the way we earn, invest, and spend our money. Sometimes it's a crisis that forces change. It may be the macro-crisis of global economic decline, or the micro-crisis of a choice we make when using a credit card at the mall. But for people whose hopes are rooted in the God revealed through Scripture, every crisis is an opportunity for God to do new work in and through our lives.

The Old Testament prophet Isaiah was writing to people caught in the cross-currents of crisis and change when he reported God's question: "I am about to do a new thing; now it springs forth, do you not perceive it?" (Isaiah 43:19). The question was not whether God could or would do a new thing, but whether the people would be prepared to perceive it. The same challenge confronts faithful people in every age.

Christ Church United Methodist is located on Park Avenue in New York City, the epicenter for the financial crisis that sank the U.S. economy in 2009. Church leaders across the country were struggling with the negative impact of the recession on their ministries. It was a precarious time to be a preacher. But in New York, speaking to those who had witnessed the crash firsthand, pastor Stephen Bauman declared his hope for the new thing that God might do in and through the witness of that congregation:

> You've heard me wonder of late if we aren't situated at a strategic cultural moment given the economic convulsions in the capital city of finance.... Though hammered by the economy, aren't we the bearers of a fresh opportunity for major reevaluation of just what makes a life worthwhile? Isn't our present moment pregnant with astonishing opportunity?[15]

The astonishing opportunity in every economic crisis is that the Spirit of God will lead us into a healthier, happier, wiser way of living at the intersection of our faith and our finances. The danger is that we will miss the new thing God wants to do. The question is always the same. Will we perceive it? Will we allow our lives to be changed?

Questions for Reflection and Discussion

1. When Crisis Forces Change

1. How have you experienced "the crisis that forces change"? Give some examples of times when you have you been forced to make major changes in the way you use your money.

2. How have you observed the two extremes of "prosperity gospel" preachers and those who are embarrassed by the subject of money? In your life at church, home, and work, what have been the predominant messages you have heard about money?

3. What are your initial impressions of John Wesley's "three plain rules"? Do they seem valid? Do they contain any surprises? Why or why not? (You can read Wesley's sermon "The Use of Money" at http://new.gbgm-umc.org/umhistory/wesley/sermons/50/.

4. What has been your experience with the book of Proverbs? Consider reading a chapter each day for thirty-one days and keeping a journal of your observations.

5. Review the "crucial elements" in the process of change as described by C. Douglas Lewis, and reflect on ways they are at

work in your life. (The elements are clarity of mission, persistent core values, and a commitment to excellence.)

6. Read Ephesians 4:17-28. How do you respond to Paul's warning?

7. Now that you have been introduced to some of John Wesley's ideas about money, what do you hope to learn or discover from this book?

2. Gain All You Can: A New Opportunity

1. What is your reaction to Jem Lugo's advice to her fellow graduates? Do you agree or disagree? Why?

2. Does Wesley's instruction to "gain all you can" surprise you? What has been your experience about the attitude of the church toward financial success?

3. How have you observed the dark side of greed in the world around you? How have you experienced it in your own life?

4. Read aloud Luke 12:13-34. How would you interpret God's judgment on the farmer? How have you seen this parable at work in our world?

5. Which of Wesley's three boundaries is most challenging for you? Why?

6. Read Proverbs 3:5-10. How have you seen this word of wisdom at work in your life?

7. If you truly followed Wesley's first rule, "Gain all you can," what changes would you make in the way you earn money?

3. Save All You Can: The New Frugality

1. Have you known anyone like Stanley Johnson? Do you identify with him? Why or why not? (You can see his commercial at http://www.youtube.com/watch?v=hn5EP9StlVA.)

2. Review Wesley's warnings about waste. What are some ways in which each of the warnings might apply to your life?

3. How have you observed or experience "shopoholism"? What have you done to break the addiction?

4. What did your parents teach you about managing money? What have you taught (or will you teach) your own children or others?

5. What does the word *frugality* mean to you? What changes would you need to make in order to live a more frugal lifestyle? What things might result?

6. Where do you find contentment? How do Paul's words about contentment connect with or contradict your experience?

7. Can you identify with the man's story at the end of the chapter? Why or why not? Are there similar ways in which you could change your own life?

4. Give All You Can: A New Generosity

1. How have you experienced "closed-fist syndrome"? (You can view the video at http://www.worshiphousemedia.com/mini-movies/13357/Closed-Fist-Syndrome.)

2. Read 1 Timothy 6:6-21. What is your first impression of

Paul's words? In what ways are they true to your own experience or observation? In what ways are they different?

3. Consider the idea that God is the "possessor" and we are "stewards." What practical differences might this idea make in your life?

4. Reflect on Wesley's four questions for the expenditure of money. What differences would they make in the ways you use money?

5. How do you respond to the author's observations about generosity? How have you seen them at work in your life? What observations would you add?

6. What is the most important lesson you have learned from this study? Consider and discuss ways in which your life and finances could be different because of it.

7. Read Isaiah 43:1-21. How do these words make you feel? What is the "new thing" God wants to do in your life?

Notes

1. When Crisis Forces Change

1. Prime Minister Gordon Brown, quoted in *Time,* April 6, 2009, 29.

2. John Harold Plumb, *England in the Eighteenth Century* (Harmondsworth: Penguin Books, 1950), 90.

3. Ellen Davis, *Getting Involved with God* (Lanham, Md.: Cowley Publications, 2001), 92.

4. John Wesley, "The Use of Money," Sermon 50, http://new.gbgm-umc.org/umhistory/wesley/sermons/50/, 2.

5. C. Douglas Lewis, "In Trust," Spring 2009, 16–18.

6. John Wesley, "The More Excellent Way," Sermon 89, http://new.gbgm-umc.org/umhistory/wesley/sermons/89/, III.1.

7. Ibid., III, 2.

8. Ibid., III, 3.

9. Charles Wesley, "Forth in Thy Name, O Lord," *The United Methodist Hymnal* (Nashville: The United Methodist Publishing House, 1989), no. 438.

10. George Eliot, *Complete Poems* (Boston: Estes and Lauriat, n.d.), 398–402.

11. Nancy Gibbs, quoted in *Time,* April 15, 2009, http://www.time.com/time/nation/article/0,8599, 1891527,00.html.

2. Gain All You Can

1. See http://www.tampabay.com/news/education/k12/article 1007369.ece.

2. John Wesley, "The Use of Money," I, 7.

3. Kurt Anderson, quoted in *Time,* April 6, 2009, 34.

4. Adam Hamilton, *Enough: Discovering Joy Through Simplicity and Generosity* (Nashville: Abingdon Press, 2009), 15–16.

5. See http://www.creditcards.com/credit-card-news/credit-card-industry-facts-personal-debt-statistics-1276.php.

6. See http://www.firstthings.com/article.php3?id_article=3838.

7. Eugene Peterson, *Christ Plays in Ten Thousand Places* (Grand Rapids: Eerdmans, 2005), 243.

8. See http://www.mindfully.org/Sustainability/Americans-Consume-24percent.htm.

9. Speech before the American Society of Newspaper Editors, April 16, 1953, http://www.quotationspage.com/quote/9556.html.

3. Save All You Can

1. See http://www.timesonline.co.uk/tol/news/world/middle_east/article6469706.ece.

2. *Tampa Tribune,* July 2, 2009, 12.

3. James A. Harnish, *Strength for the Broken Places* (Nashville: Abingdon Press, 2009), 79–80.

4. See http://en.wikiquote.org/wiki/Cat_on_a_Hot_Tin_Roof_(film).

5. See http://www.indiana.edu/~engs/hists/shop.html.

6. Skye Jethani, "Stranded in Neverland," *Christianity Today,* http://www.christianitytoday.com/le/community life/discipleship/strandedinneverland.html.

7. "The New Frugality, *Time,* http://www.time.com/time/nation/article/0,8599,1891527,00.html.

8. Lisa Earle McLeod, mail@forgetperfect.ccsend.com, 5/6/2009, personal blog.

9. Michael Maniates, quoted in *USA Today*," July 13, 2009, 1.

10. Eric Dykstra, quoted in *USA Today*.

11. Ibid.

4. *Give All You Can*

1. Hamilton, *Enough*, 96.

2. John Wesley, "The Use of Money," III, 1.

3. John Wesley, "The Danger of Riches," Sermon 87, http://new.gbgm-umc.org/umhistory/wesley/sermons/87/, I, 3–5.

4. Ibid., 3.

5. *John and Charles Wesley: Selected Writings and Hymns* (Ramsey, NJ: Paulist Press, 1981), 236.

6. John Ortberg, *When the Game Is Over, It All Goes Back in the Box* (Grand Rapids: Zondervan, 2007).

7. William Sloan Coffin Jr., "After Rocky's Death," in *Collected Sermons* (Louisville: Westminster John Knox, 2008), 193.

8. John Wesley, "The Use of Money," III, 3.

9. Ibid.

10. Ibid., III, 4.

11. Ibid., III, 5, adapted.

12. See http://www.wow4u.com/francis-bacon/index.html.

13. John Wesley, "The Use of Money," III, 6.

14. Ibid., III, 7.

15. Stephen Bauman, "The Call to Love the City," July 12, 2009, http://www.christchurchnyc.org/ser/.

Resources for Continued Study

Chilcote, Paul Wesley. *Recapturing the Wesley's Vision: An Introduction to the Faith of John and Charles Wesley.* IVP Academic, 2004.

Davis, Ellen F. *Getting Involved with God: Rediscovering the Old Testament.* Cowley Publications, 2001.

Hamilton, Adam. *Enough: Discovering Joy Through Simplicity and Generosity.* Abingdon Press, 2009.

Heitzenrater, Richard P. *Wesley and the People Called Methodist.* Abingdon Press, 1995.

Job, Rueben P. *A Wesleyan Spiritual Reader.* Abingdon Press, 1997.

Slaughter, Michael. *Upside Living in a Downside Economy.* Abingdon Press, 2009.

———. *Money Matters: Financial Freedom for All God's Children.* Abingdon Press, 2006.

Whaling, Frank (editor). *John and Charles Wesley: Selected Writings and Hymns.* Paulist Press, 1981.